TONGUES AND EXPLANATIONS

This series of short books is dedicated to the memory of my father, A. F. Pain (1915-1982).

He emerged from the Deptford slums, without education or refinement, as a natural leader of men. He was radical and traditional, patient and impetuous, obstinate and flexible, gentle and ruthless; loved or loathed by all he met. He faithfully served Christ, the church, his family and the people of Brixton.

ASHBURNHAM INSIGHTS

Tongues and Explanations

A re-reading of Scripture by

Timothy Pain

KINGSWAY PUBLICATIONS
EASTBOURNE

First published 1986

ISBN 0 86065 485 0

*Cover photo shows front water
and the main bridge at Ashburnham Place
(colour photography by Judges Postcards Ltd, Hastings).*

Printed in Great Britain for
KINGSWAY PUBLICATIONS LTD
Lottbridge Drove, Eastbourne, E. Sussex BN23 6NT by
Richard Clay (The Chaucer Press) Ltd, Bungay, Suffolk
Typeset by Nuprint Services Ltd, Harpenden, Herts AL5 4SE

Contents

Foreword to the Series

I am very pleased to commend this series of *Ashburnham Insights* which have come from the pen of Timothy Pain. Those of us who have watched developments at Ashburnham Place over the last few years have been particularly intrigued with the way things have developed. The careful thinking in these volumes comes from a background of faithful believing prayer for many years, and a deep concern for renewal and revival.

When there is an emphasis on experience, and when the subjective element in Christian living is to the fore, there is more need than ever for scriptural foundations. That is why we should be grateful to Tim for the obvious care he has taken to 'test everything', while at the same time to obey the apostolic injunction to 'despise not prophesyings'. Both should play their part in balanced Christian living.

Tim is not afraid to break new ground, and his *Insights* on speaking in tongues will be challenging to those of us who need it. I like the living way he writes, and I am sure these small books will have the wide readership they deserve.

Canon Michael Harper

Introduction

This series has been inspired by members of the Ashburnham Stable Family. This is a Christian community, part resident at Ashburnham Place (a Christian training centre) and part scattered throughout the villages and small towns of East Sussex. It is our calling to maintain an unbroken 'Chain of Prayer' within the Palladian Stable which is adjacent to Ashburnham Place. We pray, by day and night, for the renewal and spiritual unity of all Christian churches in East Sussex. It is our conviction that the hope of the world lies in the renewal of the church, and as one expression of this we have taken it upon ourselves to share in a serious re-reading of Holy Scripture.

It seems to me that much contemporary teaching is based on experience rather than the Bible. Just as the members of the Stable Family have gained courage to move away from the shallow waters of their varied experiences and traditions, so we urge you to let go and swim with Jesus in the raging torrent of living waters which is eternal life in the Spirit.

The book is humbly offered to the church as my personal re-reading with regard to tongues and explanations. It has been lived in, worked out and written down in community. It is the product of much study and prayer; reading and listening; experimentation and embarrassment; banter and disagreement. Some within the Stable Family still lovingly dissent from a few of my conclusions! Much of the material was originally worked on by the Rev. Edmund Heddle and myself for our conference weekends, when groups take time apart to be with God.

In recent years God has called the Stable Family to new depths of prayer and praise. These I humbly share. They are not the last words on tongues. Those can never be written. What follows is simply a statement of where God has led this community—thus far. It is our fervent hope and prayer that God will lead us 'farther up and farther in', so that this book becomes an embarrassment to us because of its shallowness and inevitable errors.

These *Ashburnham Insights* have been written with housegroup leaders in mind. One of the great works of the Spirit in the last fifteen years has been the emergence and establishment of house groups. It is my prayer that these four books will aid these leaders in their high and holy calling.

I have tried to write in a way that is simple enough to satisfy the sincere seeker, but is sufficiently thorough to persuade those called to teach and lead in the church. The scripture references should all be looked up and examined as you proceed through the text. Bible quotations are normally taken from the Jerusalem Bible.

Any plaudits should be shared between John and Marlis Bickersteth, Helen Brown, Winifred Cox, Edmund Heddle, Gay Hyde, Jo and Susie Marriott, Margery May, Dennis and Pat Nolan, Alan Pain, Barbara Stidwill, Muriel Teideman, Roger and Penny Willcock and my wife Alison. Their prayers, patience, comments, advice, encouragement, work and love have brought the Insights from gestation to publication.

Timothy Pain

The renewal lives by the re-reading of the New Testament.

Cardinal Suenens

Back to the Bible or back to the jungle.

Luis Palau

Forbid not to speak in tongues.

St Paul

Plenteous of grace, descend from high
Rich in Thy sevenfold energy!
Thou strength of His Almighty hand
Whose power does Heaven and earth command,
Proceeding Spirit, our defence,
Who dost the gift of tongues dispense,
And crown'st Thy gifts with eloquence!

John Dryden

It is a language of freedom.... He who speaks it exists in tomorrow's world. Tomorrow becomes today, and the jubilant speaker experiences the beauty which some day will redeem the world.... It is the Sabbath of language, a Sabbath made for man.

Rudolf Bohren

What Is the Gift of Tongues?

I suspect there has been more controversy over the gift of tongues than over any other aspect of charismatic renewal. There has certainly been much antagonism towards this precious gift, and many foolish claims about it, for nigh on two thousand years. Many will have heard of the fictitious man who was allegedly caught blaspheming in Chinese. Yet despite all the hot air and red ink the gift of tongues has a very low public profile. It is rarely heard in public worship; it is virtually non-existent in evangelism; and it is impossible to measure its use in private devotions. After questioning thousands of our conference visitors, I know that most people, following an initial rush of enthusiasm and blessing, allow the gift to lapse. My surmise is that this is related to the fact that very few have ever heard a sermon on tongues. The purpose and practice of this holy discipline is rarely taught from the pulpits of our country.

Several years ago I began a systematic reading and evaluation of published works on tongues. With the exception of Morton Kelsey's classic volume, *Tongue speaking*,[1] the authors of these books seem to base their understanding of spiritual gifts in general, and tongues in particular, around the Pentecostal understanding. This was set out in 1934 by Harold Horton in *The gifts of the Spirit*,[2] and in Protestantism little fresh thought or experimentation appears to have taken place since then.

This book is simply a placing on record of my thoughts. I hope they will lead to further study, experimentation and correspondence. I lay no claim to divine inspiration, only to creative insights. It is my prayer that one result will be a revaluation by leaders of their practice and understanding of tongues.

There is a common tendency to try to make Scripture fit our personal experience when these two forces clash. But our experience is fallible, whereas Scripture is not. Blessing is no measure of doctrine for we have a God who delights to bless even when we are in error. So please allow Scripture to scorch your ideas and experiences. I pray that you will be blessed and stretched as you think through what the Scriptures say about tongues, and what I think the Scriptures teach about tongues.

A miracle

The spiritual gift of tongues is a miracle. It occurs when a human being prays to God in a language he has never learnt, and that must be a miracle! Let me put it another way; the gift of tongues is a supernatural phenomenon. It is God the Holy Spirit providing men with words they cannot understand in order that they may speak more effectively to God their Father. Untainted as it is by the human mind, it may well be the purest form of worship this side of heaven. The gift of tongues is part of the continuing ministry of the Holy Spirit and, as such, it glorifies or illuminates Jesus. Yet it is often maligned and misunderstood, despised and rejected, frequently forbidden and commonly misused.

Its importance

Tongue speakers are sometimes accused of making much of little. It is suggested that the gift of tongues is a minor irrelevancy, a Corinthian aberration tucked away in a half-verse here and there. Yet the New Testament contains more about tongues than baptism, more even than about the eucharist.

There are five important passages of Scripture which need to be examined and these should be re-read most carefully: Mark 16:15–20, Acts 2:1–13, Acts 10:44–48, Acts 19:1–7, 1 Corinthians 11:2–14:40.

The language

It appears that the gift of tongues is the equipping of a saint with an unlearnt language. This language is given by the Holy Spirit who then enables that believer to enunciate words. It is not just sounds. Sounds may precede words, as in all language development; but language, with proper syntax, will quickly follow. Those who cheaply dismiss tongues as 'gibberish' have not carefully examined the painstaking research and study from many centuries and in traditions other than their own.

A sign

In Mark 16:17 Jesus said that tongues would be one of the five signs which would accompany those preaching the gospel. This means that it is a sign given by Almighty God to confirm the truth of the proclaimed word. So the gift of tongues should have a special place in bringing unbelievers to faith in Christ. Paul emphasized this in 1 Corinthians 14:22, and it was seen at Pentecost when the praise and mystery of the tongues were part of the challenge to the crowd. We will note in a later section the wide use of tongues in evangelism through the Middle Ages. My experience is that time and again unbelievers are entranced by tongues, especially solo sung tongues. They regularly ask more questions about this gift than either healings or prophecy. There have been many discussions about tongues at our local public house, some into the small hours; and I can identify individuals who came to belief partly through their appreciation of the beauty of tongues used correctly in public worship.

Its value as evidence

The apostles, in Acts 10:44–48, accepted the gift of tongues as an evidence that the Gentile household of Cornelius had received Holy Spirit. It is not the only evidence, and neither is it essential, as some have misconstrued it, but merely one among several evidences. The person who has not been filled with Holy Spirit, by Jesus, will not speak in tongues. This gift is reserved for those who have been immersed in the baptistry of the Holy Spirit.

There is a demonic counterfeit of tongues which can be seen in every false religion and in many occult practices. I would have thought that this should underline the existence and importance of a godly reality. One weak point of Morton Kelsey's excellent work is his failure to distinguish between true and false religions. It is to be regretted that he includes Mormonism in his church history section.

A gift from God

Paul taught that tongues is a gift available to all believers (1 Corinthians 14:5) to enhance their prayers and worship, and a gift given to the church to build it up in public worship and to challenge unbelievers. This public gift may be given to any church member, but will be given most frequently to a selected few, who can be described as having received a ministry in tongues. From the way this gift is received and developed we can see that tongues is the product of divine and human co-operation: on our side, we cannot invent a language and God, on his side, does not impose the language against our will. We provide the vocal chords, breath, tongue, palate, teeth and lips; the Holy Spirit supplies the words. We move our speech-making mechanism and as the Spirit suggests the words, so we speak them out. Volume, speed, starting and stopping—all are under our control.

New and other

This gift is described as 'new' tongues in Mark 16:17 and as 'other' tongues in Acts 2:4. In the Greek, this is *kainos* not *neos*, and *heteros* not *allos*. This means it is new, not in the sense of never having been heard before, but new to the speaker, different from the language he is accustomed to using.

Angels

A particular tongue may not necessarily be a known human language. 1 Corinthians 13:1 suggests the possibility that it might be an angelic language. The thought of speaking in the language of Michael and Gabriel is not to be taken lightly: picture the exciting possibility of joining with the cherubim and seraphim, of participating on earth in their heavenly worship. At times this does appear to happen in corporate singing with the spirit. A clear change can be noticed when human languages and music seem to be replaced by something extra-terrestrial. This might appear fanciful, but a large enough number of non-Christians has described it as 'angelic' to make me take it seriously.

Fire

Acts 2:3 describes the tongues as 'tongues of fire'. In the Old Testament fire fell upon the altar of the newly built Temple to ignite the offering—thus demonstrating its acceptance by God. Tongues of fire fall upon believers today to set us apart for ministry and to ignite us for action. This gift has been a trigger releasing many people into supernatural devotion and service, and is often a conscious experience of assurance. Many testify that at the moment the gift was given they received an overwhelming conviction of their worthiness in Christ and their adoption by God.

Prayer without ceasing

What follows is a 'creative guess' based on John 4:14. Jesus indicated that the living water he was to give—which we understand to be the Spirit—would continually well up inside the believer. This alludes to Psalm 36:9 and Isaiah 58:11. Is it too much to suggest that the gift of tongues is one facet of this fountain bubbling up inside us, offering light and praise to Jesus? Speaking or singing in tongues would then merely be the adjustment in volume to make audible this inner, everlasting bubbling.

The Direction of Tongues

1 Corinthians 14:2 is quite unambiguous: 'Anybody with the gift of tongues speaks to God, but not to other people.' Tongues is always God-ward in its direction. It is never man-ward. Edward O'Connor in *A Catholic Pentecostal Movement* states:

> Speaking in tongues is a mode of prayer, not a means of communication. The one who speaks in tongues addresses God not man. What he says is not understood either by himself or by those around him. However, if someone knows the language they will, but that is quite accidental.[3]

David Du Plessis in *Glossolalia* adds:

> It seems clear that Paul considered all speaking in tongues as prayer and always addressed to God. . . . never as a message to man.[4]

Therefore the explanation/interpretation will always be in the form of a prayer or praise. Man speaking to God and not God speaking to man. In an earlier age Tertullian wrote:

> Let him produce a psalm, a vision, a prayer, whenever an interpretation of tongues occurs to him.[5]

Throughout church history until 1830 the gift of tongues was always understood as prayer and praise. The God-ward direction never varied. It was Edward Irving and the Catholic Apostolic Church who first confused tongues with prophecy. Their error was absorbed into Pentecostalism and so today much is made of 'messages' in tongues. However, a careful re-reading of Harold Horton's chapter on interpretation in *The Gifts of the Spirit* is most instructive. Though he uses the word 'message', his understanding of the correct context and essential direction of an explanation/interpretation appears to be identical to my own and contrary to that of most who profess to follow him.[6]

I disagree with Bishop David Pytches' statement in *Renewal* magazine that 'Tongues and interpretation = prophecy or a 'word of knowledge' or a 'word of wisdom''[7] and also with Canon Michael Green who wrote in *I believe in Satan's downfall* that: 'God can guide a congregation with immediacy through a message in tongues that is then interpreted.'[8] Surely the Scriptures make it plain that there can be no such thing as a 'message' in tongues?

It is ludicrous to think of Almighty God, who has at his disposal Holy Scripture, the gift of prophecy, the gift of the word of knowledge and even angelic messengers, choosing to speak in a celestial code which needs to be cracked. In 1 Corinthians 14:29 Paul took pains to teach that a revelation from God to men must be discerned/separated/sifted by those prophets who have not spoken. Can it be that God would send a message to stand unsifted in breach of these orders? This is most implausible. Yet the common practice today is for a tongue to remain uninterpreted with a subsequent prophecy being deemed the explanation. This means that the church misses out on edification; God misses out on glorification; unbelievers miss out on clarification and charismatic critics have a field day at the contemporary non-New Testament use of gifts. Critical writers frequently home in on the absurdity of 'messages', quote an example when, supposedly, the

Sutton Coldfield Baptist Church, W. Midlands

On Sunday, March 31st 1985, Lyn Pain, the minister's wife and leader of the music, sang a solo song in tongues in the course of evening worship. Her husband, Alan, who was leading the service at the time, felt that he had received the explanation of this tongue and, somewhat tentatively, offered it in the form of a prayer.

However, many in the congregation did not realize that this prayer had been given as the explanation to the tongue, and a few minutes later, towards the end of the service, a lady came to the front. She read out an explanation, which she had written down, to the song sung earlier in tongues. Its harmony with Alan's explanation was striking and, on impulse, Alan asked the congregation to sit down.

He informed them that his earlier prayer had been intended as the explanation, commented on the marked similarity between the two explanations, and then asked any others who had had a similar 'impression' to raise a hand. Between fifteen and twenty people raised a hand. There were men and women of all stages of Christian experience.

Alan was thus able to show them that they had not merely had an impression, but had received from the Lord the charismatic gift of 'explanation'. It was an extremely valuable opportunity to encourage them to boldness for the future, and also a uniquely valuable object lesson for the whole church, especially those who were wary because they had felt that these things lacked any spiritual objectivity.

'translation' was wrong and then smugly dance away to ditch the baby of tongues with the bath-water of messages.

This is not to say that an explanation—an adoration, a prayer, a praise—may not be used by God to convey a message, for example, an explanation containing the phrase, 'Oh promise-keeping God, we praise your holy name', might be the very word to aid someone struggling with an unfulfilled promise. However, the explanation in itself would have been a prayer of praise to a promise-keeping God, not a message from God to remind us that he keeps his word. When a 'message' has occurred I am not suggesting that a false explanation has been brought, rather that no explanation has been given but a person with a prophecy has spoken too soon and everybody has assumed that this prophecy was the explanation. Prophets should exercise self-control and wait until a God-ward explanation has been brought before speaking out their edifying man-ward message from God.

In groups honestly and seriously seeking authentic explanations it appears that a beauty of language, a lyricism, a poeticism is discovered which is stunningly lovely. At times, long-forgotten liturgy from another age or tradition is poured out. The explanation of a tongue can have an effect on unbelievers similar to the effect of the beautiful song in Song of Solomon 5:10–16 which caused those listening to cry out, 'Which way did your beloved turn, so that we can help you look for him?' (6:1). It would be pointless to transcribe a tongue, but I can give you an example of an explanation. Rather than select the best, I will simply record the most recent at the time of writing this first draft. This is a word for word rendering of the explanation which God gave to an octogenarian evangelical Anglican lay reader on January 31st 1985 in the Great Hall of Ashburnham Place. It is not a translation of the preceding tongue. It is the Spirit-inspired gist of a mystery which is unutterable in English.

It's a time for celebration
For our prayers have all been heard;
It's a day of jubilation
And our God has kept his word;

There are tongues, interpretations,
And his prophecies unfold.
There are miracles of healing
As there were in days of old—

For our Lord, our Christ is with us
And his Spirit falls in power
And we are lost in wonder,
Who share this precious hour.

So it's a time for celebration
Thanks for prayers that have been heard,
It's our day of jubilation
For our God has kept his word.

Father Rene Laurentin records two particularly helpful stories in his excellent book *Catholic Pentecostalism.*[9] The first time a Father Regimbal spoke in tongues:

> Two orthodox priests dressed as laymen immediately recognised the prayer as part of Orthodox Greek liturgy in the last century, but later eliminated. The two priests had studied at the same seminary at Athens and had been particularly struck by the Trinitarian doxology which had come up in their course on the history of the liturgy. They could not understand hearing it on my lips (in Quebec) and in the very dialect of their own native village!

On one occasion when Father Regimbal sung in tongues an elderly Baptist pastor broke down in tears and said:

> The song you were singing is a Hebrew Christian song from the fourth century, and when I myself was a student in Jerusalem, this was one of the songs used to prove there had been a Christian community in Jerusalem at that time. It's a

> song about the Prince of Peace. You used the words and music I learnt in Jerusalem.[10]

To speak or sing in tongues is to bring glorious praise or devoted prayer to Almighty God. It is not an incomprehensible second-class telegram misdirected to the wrong continent by some bungling angel!

Some Common Misunderstandings

It is not a linguistic ability

The gift of tongues was not, and is not, a short cut to communication in missionary work. Tongues was not necessarily the language of whichever people the disciples were preaching to. The crowds on the day of Pentecost heard the disciples praising God in their own languages, but when Peter preached he used his native tongue—Aramaic. The alleged examples in history are based on the unprovable presupposition that the tongue content was preaching.

St Vincent Ferrer, a Dominican known as the 'Angel of the Judgement', travelled across Europe from 1399 to 1419. He converted people in the Alpine regions of Switzerland, in Brittany, Flanders, Savoy, Lyons, Genoa, Lombardy and all along the route between these places. He seldom remained in any place for more than one day. Most biographers hold that he was endowed with tongues and that it was the exercise of this gift which led to the large numbers of conversions and miracles. Morton Kelsey proposes Ferrer to be the closest example found to Acts 2, but misses the point that what the Pentecost crowds heard in their own language was praise, not preaching.[11] The late Eric Hutchings told me that in Belgium just after the Second

World War he experienced a one-off gift of tongues, as a result of which a number of people were converted. He believed he had preached in Flemish, but this cannot be proved. His deduction was based on his premise that salvation can only come from hearing preaching. Eric did not recognize the place of praise tongues as a sign to unbelievers.

My contention is that in these and similar incidents the tongue content was praise and worship, not preaching. Of course there are times when there may be little variation in content between the two, but the direction and aim is quite different.

It is not a psychological abnormality

Speaking in tongues is not an ejaculation from the subconscious. It is not a result of suggestion, nor linked to schizophrenia, catalepsy or hysteria. The fact that tongues have been noted among the insane does not prove that all who speak in tongues are insane! Dr James Packer writes patronizingly of the gift of tongues in *Keep in Step with the Spirit*, comparing them to, 'yodelling in the Alps and warbling under the shower', but graciously concedes that, 'It is not a product of the kind of disassociation of mind and bodily function that argues stress, repression or mental sickness.'[12] The sheer lack of emotion or excitement in tongues means that it is a great disappointment to those seeking a spiritual thrill instead of an aid to deeper prayer.

It is not a miracle of hearing

Some suggest that the miracle of tongues does not take place in the mouth of the speaker, but rather in the ear of the hearer. This idea was first suggested and rejected as far back as A.D. 350. If it were true, why did the Acts 2 crowd suggest that the disciples were drunk?

My experience is that this suggestion is incorrect. I live in a multi-lingual community, where the gift of tongues is frequently used. We have never experienced a simultaneous aural translation among ourselves, nor in the course of my research, have I ever heard of anybody else receiving such a thing.

It is not a restricted gift

Some, who correctly suggest that the 'Do all?' of 1 Corinthians 12:29–30 presumes the answer 'No', go on to assume incorrectly that this means speaking in tongues is not for all, but is only for an unfortunate few! But 1 Corinthians 12:27–30 refers to the structure of ministry in the church. It emphasizes the plurality of ministry by listing nine different categories of ministry. Four of these—healings, tongues, miracles and explanations—result from the development of a particular Spirit-given gift within an individual. Paul's implied 'No' is in reply to his questions whether all believers will speak publicly in tongues during the public worship of the church and whether all the apostles, prophets and teachers etc will of necessity also have a public ministry in miracles, healing and tongues. His 'No' does not suggest that only a restricted number of believers will be able to worship privately in tongues. It seems to me that in 1 Corinthians 14:5 Paul demonstrates a belief that it is possible for all to speak in tongues. This echoes Jesus' statement in Mark 16:17.

As at Pentecost, the Holy Spirit does give this gift to some who have not sought it, just as some are spontaneously healed and others are unexpectedly filled with Holy Spirit. However, as in every area of the Christian life, it is normally those who have kept on asking, seeking and knocking who have received. A lack of importunity, rather than a surfeit of divine indifference, is the most common reason for the absence of this precious gift.

The gift of tongues for public worship referred to in 1 Corinthians 12 and 14 is not to be sought by an individual, but claimed by each church. This might be restricted to a few—maybe a different few at every service—but private prayer tongues is unrestricted. It is available to all those who are living in the baptistry of the Holy Spirit.

Crofton Park Baptist Church, London

Over a period of several years, Robert Allen, the minister of this inner-city church, had given teaching on spiritual gifts, but there was little public use of them. Slowly it dawned on him that teaching was not enough. He had to be willing to lead the people into them. This came to a head in October 1983 at a church residential weekend away.

Robert had prayed privately in tongues for some years, but was petrified at the thought of bringing a tongue to the church. He says, 'I was afraid of what people would think. I was even more afraid my "gift" would be exposed as false. During that weekend the Lord spoke clearly about this and I shared it with Paul Harris, the guest speaker. Almost immediately a deacon, whom I trusted deeply, approached me to suggest I should speak publicly in a tongue! At the first service I knew I must pray in tongues and was as frightened as I have ever been in my life. At a space in the service I began to speak; sentences came with expression and feelings and I knew I was talking to the Lord. The words were strange, yet I was dimly aware of what I was saying. Paul Harris brought an explanation which was one of the most beautiful prayers I have ever heard—about walking on the edge of a precipice and being frightened of falling.'

There were two results. The explanation deeply affected a married woman who was contemplating an affair. She felt God had looked into her soul and expressed the cry of her heart. She wept; and went home to mend her damaged marriage.

The more obvious effect was on the service. The flood-gates opened. People who had never done so, prophesied. There was another tongue and explanation. God's love washed over the church; some sobbed; others hugged; and there came a profound sense of God's presence. That weekend changed the church, and now more and more people regularly bring something for and from the Lord both in business meetings and at the Sunday services.

It is not demonic in origin

The Rituale Romanum, of circa A.D. 1000 established speaking in demonic tongues as one of the three vital evidences which demonstrate a need for the ministry of exorcism and blessing. (The others are preternatural strength and a knowledge of facts beyond the education or experience of the individual.) These demonic tongues do exist. Many have heard them, including myself. However, it does not follow from their existence that all tongues must be demonic in origin. The person who has been filled with Holy Spirit is not going to utter demonic tongues. 1 Corinthians 12:3 makes this quite plain.

It is not an involuntary act

The myth is still perpetuated that the gift of tongues is 'ecstatic'. Some older Pentecostals understood it as an involuntary manifestation attesting Spirit baptism, but this was mainly due to their attempt to root tongues in the Old Testament. Many works published before 1960 present tongues as an ecstatic act, but most books written since the advent of the charismatic movement refute this notion. We have complete control over the phenomenon. This is why tongues can be suppressed. We can adjust the volume and vary the speed. Most people can pray in tongues without making an audible noise. (The words are formed in the usual way, with the tongue moving rapidly, but the lips are not opened, thus preventing the sound from being heard.) Of course, public muttering in tongues can be extremely irritating and it is this which conveys the impression that speaking in tongues is involuntary. I suggest that this habit be discouraged.

It is not a dispensational feature

A few argue that the gift of tongues ceased when the New Testament was completed and feebly point to 1 Corinthians 13:8 as vague support. But this would also mean that all knowledge had ceased 1900 years ago. It is not a credible idea. This verse refers to the perfection that will be ours at the second coming of Christ. The gift of tongues has been a feature of every century and every branch of the church. It has never ceased. The following section demonstrates the truth of this statement.

Tongues Through the Ages

First century

The New Testament contains enough examples of the gift of tongues to convince us of its use. We need not look elsewhere.

Second century

Polycarp, the Bishop of Smyrna, appears to have prayed in tongues at his martyrdom in A.D. 155. The record of this was compiled by Marcion, from eye witnesses, within one year of Polycarp's death. Irenaeus, the Bishop of Lyons, wrote in *Against Heresies*: 'In like manner we do also hear many brethren in the Church who possess prophetic gifts, and who through the Spirit speak all kind of languages.'[13] In this century Montanus of Phrygia and his followers were famous (or infamous, depending on your point of view!) for their use of tongues.

Third century

Novatian of Rome, who gave the western church its first major document on the Holy Trinity, wrote: 'This is he who places prophets in the church, instructs teachers, directs tongues...'[14] We have already referred on page 17 to Tertullian of Carthage's teaching on the gift of tongues.

Fourth century

There is good evidence that Hilary, Bishop of Poitiers, Ambrose, Bishop of Milan and the Egyptian Abbot, St Pachomius, all spoke in tongues. John Chrysostom, fourth century Bishop of Constantinople, and Augustine, Bishop of Hippo are often quoted to support the theory that tongues had died out (and jolly well ought to have stayed died out!). Yet both Pachomius and Ambrose gave clear evidence that this gift was still common in their localities at exactly the time when Chrysostom asserted that tongues: 'Now no longer takes place.'[15] Chrysostom simply did not hear tongues occur.

Fifth century

Augustine's famous down-grading of tongues in his *Confessions* was written between A.D. 397 and A.D. 401. But twenty years later in *City of God* he repudiated much of what he had earlier written on gifts and miracles. In A.D. 427 he wrote:

> This record and attesting, in fact, is what I took care to have done, once I realised how many miracles were occurring in our own day and which were so like the miracles of old.... It is only two years ago that the keeping of records was begun here in Hippo.[16]

Sixth to fourteenth centuries

There is no clear recorded instance of the gift of tongues in the western church from the fall of Rome until St Hildegard in the twelfth century. The most probable example is Caedmon, the first English poet, at Whitby Abbey.

Demonic tongues were frequently attested to in this period and it is possible that some of the many executed partly for tongue speaking were godly people.

It is well established that this gift was in constant use in the eastern church from the fall of Rome to the fall of Constantinople. Many within the Greek Orthodox Church, including the Patriarch of Constantinople, maintain that the gift of tongues never ceased among their monastic orders. The *Encyclopaedia Britannica* reports that western mendicant friars prayed in tongues during the thirteenth century.[17] However, it was St Vincent Ferrer, referred to on page 23, who was essentially used in the fourteenth century to re-quicken a western Christian understanding that the gift of tongues could be divine as well as demonic.

Fifteenth, sixteenth and seventeenth centuries

During this period two famous saints—St Francis Xavier and St Lewis Bertrand—were canonized with the gift of tongues being listed as one of the reasons for this honour. Both of their lives merit serious study by those acquainted only with evangelical revivals. The Abbess Colette of Corbi, never canonized, appears to have prayed in tongues, as does St Peter of Alcantara.

By far the most famous user of tongues in this period was St Teresa of Avila (though there is some evidence that Luther received tongues two years before his final monastic vows). Teresa's famous description of tongues, in her autobiography, remains one of the loveliest in history:

> I don't know any other terms for describing it or explaining it. Nor does the soul then know what to do, whether to speak or to be silent, whether to laugh or to weep. This prayer is a glorious foolishness, a heavenly madness where the true wisdom is learned; and it is for the soul a most delightful way of enjoying.[18]

She called tongues 'a language that belongs to heaven'.

The gift of tongues was common among the French Calvinists (Huguenots) for two centuries. This culminated in an extraordinary incident at the beginning of the eighteenth century when more than three hundred children aged between three and ten, from all over Cevennes, prophesied and spoke in tongues with astonishing power and accuracy. This move of God's Spirit continued for over ten years but was forcibly subdued by the French Army in 1711 and a considerable number of the children were either executed or transported.

The Quakers were the first to speak in tongues in North America and were the most controversial group in Britain to do so. William Burrough, an early Quaker, wrote in *Preface to Great Mystery*, 'We received after the pouring down of the Spirit upon us, and our mouths opened, and we spake with new tongues as the Lord gave us utterance.'[19]

Eighteenth century

Tongues was common among the Jansenists in France. They were a Catholic holiness sect which reacted against the harshness of the Jesuits. The gift was also seen among the Methodists in England. Thomas Walsh, one of Wesley's right-hand men, wrote in his diary on 8th March 1750: 'This morning the Lord gave me a language I knew not of, raising my soul to Him in a wondrous manner.'[20] It was a feature of the Shakers in North America as well as in England; and was common among the Moravians in Germany, and wherever their amazing world-wide missionary activity took them.

An anonymous critic of Count Zinzendorf and the Moravians penned what must be one of the most eloquent denunciations of tongues ever made: 'He and his followers were great dealers in the Spirit and affected strange convulsive heavings, and unnatural postures. And in one of these fits they commonly broke into some disconnected Jargon, which they often passed upon the vulgar as the exuberant and resistless evacuations of the Spirit, and many other such enthusiastic stuff.'[21]

But the Moravians were the true charismatics of their day. Revival came to North America and Britain as a direct consequence of their phenomenal intercession, much of which was in tongues.

Nineteenth century

The gift of tongues achieved notoriety in England through Edward Irving and the Catholic Apostolic Church. Large numbers of the London gentry and many leading intellectuals of the day visited his Regent Square Church to hear the tongues.

Men as theologically diverse as Pastor Blumhardt and the Curé D'Ars ministered with the aid of tongues. The gift was authenticated in countries as far apart as Russia, Sweden, North America, France, Germany and India. From the 1870s onwards, tongues was a feature of the American revivalism which led to Pentecostalism.

Twentieth century

In the first half of this century the gift of tongues was mainly contained within the spreading Pentecostal Church and the emerging national Christian movements in the third world. Since 1960 the Holy Spirit has restored this precious gift within every tradition, culture and denomination across the world. Never before has such a paean risen to heaven.

Throughout the ages those who have prayed in tongues have been criticized, exorcized, excommunicated and even executed. The devil would have it so. Tongues is to the fallen heavenly choirmaster as fingernails scraping down a blackboard is to me. How he must hate the glorious praise that resounds around the globe in this our day!

The Upbuilding of the Church

For the last eighty-five years, most of the thinking about the gift of tongues has been focused on its function as an evidence of personal baptism in Holy Spirit. Its use as a sign in evangelism has been ignored (can you imagine tongues at a Billy Graham rally?) and only minimal attention has been given to understanding its place in the local church. These aspects need prayerful study and bold experimentation. In the New Testament, most emphasis is placed on the role of tongues in the edification of a local church. We must give this our close attention.

In 1 Corinthians 11–15 Paul gave detailed teaching about the public worship of a local church. These chapters about worship stress the centrality of the eucharist, the place of women, the primacy of love and the need for spiritual gifts to be exercised in the worship services of a local church. It is incorrect to apply these four to individuals or to a counselling situation. The key verb of chapter 14 is *oikodomeo*. This is most commonly translated as 'to edify', but is better rendered 'to build'. We can understand this more fully by the phrase 'to build together in order to build up'. If we desire the upbuilding of the church we must pay special attention to 1 Corinthians 14. The following lessons, about the gift of tongues in public worship, are deduced from this chapter.

1. The individual who brings a public prayer in tongues during a meeting is himself built up (verse 4).

2. It is desirable and possible for all to use this gift in public (verse 5).

3. An 'interpretation' (verse 5) is not a translation. The Greek verb *diermeneuo* means 'to explain fully'. It is the word used in Luke 24:27 to describe Christ's explaining of the Scriptures on the Emmaus road. I use the word 'explanation' rather than 'interpretation', as the latter creates the wrong impression that a tongue is translatable. The explanation is the Spirit-imparted 'gist' of a tongue: I have given an example of such an explanation on page 21. It is important to repeat that a tongue is a mystery which cannot be uttered in earthly words, so it is not to be expected that the explanation will be a word for word translation. The explainer listens to God for what he is to say, not to the tongue to guess the style and theme. This means that a sung tongue is not necessarily followed by a sung explanation, nor a long tongue by an explanation of equivalent length. Tertullian—one of the church fathers of the second century—wrote that the explanation could be a psalm, a prayer or a vision. Horton suggested it could be: 'pictorial, parabolic, descriptive or literal'.[22]

4. Prayer in tongues followed by the explanation builds together and builds up the local church. Some still offer the stale and hoary equation, 'tongues + explanation = prophecy'. As we have seen (page 18), this is not so. Verse 5 shows that tongues plus explanation is of equivalent value to prophecy, but it is not the equivalent of prophecy. Both build up the local church but verses 2 and 3 show that they do this from opposite directions. Prophecies, as communication, must be separated and sifted. Explanations, as worship, are received without comment.

5. The explanation, rather than the tongue, should be concentrated upon, as this is the element which upbuilds the local church (verse 5).

6. Praise and prayer in tongues should not be brought

Susie Marriott—a member of St Peter's, Ashburnham, E. Sussex

Susie, a housewife, was converted quietly and slowly during 1971. She was filled with Holy Spirit in 1976 when, at her request, her vicar laid hands on her. She experienced a real sense of peace, but had no expectation of tongues. Her daughter and husband were then converted, filled with Holy Spirit, and both almost immediately received tongues. Very many people laid hands on, and prayed for Susie to receive tongues—to no effect. She asked persistently and, in September 1979, eventually started to pray in tongues.

Susie first prayed publicly in tongues during 1981 at a very small prayer group. She was terrified. Over two years passed before she gained courage to pray in tongues at a larger, more formal service. Her heart always thumped away beforehand. The breakthrough came in January 1984 when she began to sing in tongues. Rapidly the gift developed into a remarkable ministry. Today, Susie is regularly required to sing or speak in tongues during services and meetings. She has even been prompted to sing in tongues at a funeral and a large special anniversary celebration, but she never uses the gift where she is unknown to the leaders.

She often knows several days in advance that she should use this gift. A tune will float through her mind, but she does not rehearse the tongue. She prepares herself to be ready to offer it at the right moment.

Before her tongue at the funeral service, she had asked permission of both the widow and the vicar; and had then established that somebody would be present with an explanation. Today there is no fear, only demonic suggestions like, 'Why bother?' or, 'You're showing off!' or, 'It's the same old tune' (it never is).

Susie is constantly thrilled by the reactions of non-Christians—especially to sung tongues. People always thank her and comment on its beauty. One elderly Christian, on hearing a tongue for the first time, commented, 'I would love a recording. It sounded like a plaintive Russian song from the Steppes. Beautiful!'

during worship without an explanation (verses 6–12). This must cause some rethinking of the contemporary phenomenon which is normally called 'singing in the Spirit', but is more accurately described as 'singing with the spirit'. (All singing should be 'in the Spirit', but only tongues is 'with the spirit'.) In most gatherings there is no explanation after congregational singing with the spirit and no seeking of one from God. This cannot be correct. Corporate singing with the spirit is unexplained only because few leaders expect, ask or make the space for God to provide one. I deal with this more fully on pages 55-58.

7. Those who have received the gift of tongues should pray for the gift of explanation (verse 13).

8. We should not become unbalanced and pray only with the mind—or only in tongues. There should be the four-fold balance in public worship of prayer with the mind and prayer in tongues, singing praise with the mind and singing praise in tongues (verse 15).

9. We have freedom of choice in deciding whether to pray in tongues or in our natural language (verse 15).

10. Prayer and praise in tongues can be an expression of thanksgiving (verse 16).

11. The gift of tongues is a sign for unbelievers (verse 22).

12. This gift was important to Paul and was well used by him (verse 18).

13. Our motive in bringing the praise of prayer in tongues should be to benefit the church, not to draw attention to ourselves (verse 26).

14. We should, in the days before a service, ask God what contribution he has for us to bring to the public worship. God wants 'everyone' to be ready with their God-assigned contribution. The church has fallen into two equal and opposite errors. Either, the priest/minister prepares thoroughly, under the Spirit's guidance, everything that will take place or, the congregation and leaders trust that God will spontaneously inspire any or all at the meeting. It

is unfortunate that in correctly ejecting the one-man band, thorough preparation has also been thrown out of the window. It appears that the normal procedure should be that those to whom God has revealed their particular part of the meeting—including a tongue or explanation—should intimate this to the leader. He, by means of the gift of wisdom, then prepares the order of the service.

The detail of an explanation, or a prompting that we will be required to bring, can be given before the tongue has been brought, even before the meeting. It is our custom for people to telephone the leaders the day before the meeting with their God-given contributions. People come to our meetings ready (sometimes!) with a tongue, or explanation (and all the other component parts of worship). They are either announced: 'Joe will now sing the tongue of praise the Lord prompted him about this morning and then Penny will bring the explanation she received in a vision last Wednesday'; or they are informed of the place in the service when they should bring their contribution. We still leave space for extemporary spiritual gifts, but they fit into the framework which has been prepared with the help of the gift of wisdom.

I do not expect people to rehearse spiritual gifts, but rather to prepare themselves thoroughly before worship. 1 Corinthians 11–14 suggests many aspects of this vital preparation, one of which is that we seriously ask God whether he would have us contribute any part of the worship at the forthcoming meeting. God may prompt us to suggest a hymn or reading, to give out books or sit in a particular place, or to be ready to speak a tongue or prophecy. It is these promptings which are mentioned to the leaders. However, God is fully aware that beginners often need more than a prompting and he sometimes supplies the full details of the gift in advance.

When I first began to preach I wrote out sermons in full; now I use fewer notes. I know several folk who used to write out prophecies before a meeting, but now with more experience no longer need to do so. It is exactly the same with tongues and explanations. Some rehearse the God-given tune of a sung tongue, but not the words. Others gain their initial courage by repeating the tongue. Surely God can give the same tongue more than once.

A few people have a difficulty with the notion of receiving an explanation before a tongue, as if this makes the tongue redundant. Other people think that an explanation automatically makes the preceding tongue superfluous. 'Why the tongue?' they say. 'Why not just the explanation?'

There are two answers. Firstly, though the two gifts do make a complete unit, each element has a specialist, unique function. The tongue is a sign to unbelievers—not believers—and the explanation builds up the church—but not unbelievers. Taken together, they glorify God. Secondly, the gifts are presented in the context of the 'body' teaching. Each gift always requires another gift before it is complete. This is to underline the point that no minister, no individual, is omnicompetent. The explanation needs a tongue, and the tongue needs an explanation. Together they make a whole. Which is received first is neither here nor there, but they do need to be delivered in the right order. It does not matter whether I pick up a screwdriver before a screw, but having picked them up there is really only one way round that makes any sense.

15. Extemporary prayer and praise in tongues during public worship is not sanctioned in 1 Corinthians 14. The presence of the 'explainer' must be established *before* a tongue is brought. Those painful pauses which follow a tongue, full of agonized, silent 'please let it be somebody else, Lord' prayers, can be eradicated if the biblical pattern of preparation is followed.

The only acceptable place for spontaneous tongues is in a local church where several people have been given clearly recognized ministries of explanation. Spontaneous tongues can be brought if one of these people is present (verse 28). This is not a charter for clergy to discourage tongues in 'their' services, but rather a sound framework for a more frequent use of this precious gift.

16. The leader of the meeting must ensure that no more than three people speak or sing in tongues. These three can bring several contributions during the meeting (verse 27). I felt we were beginning to move from the problems of death to the problems of life when I first had to state gently that only David, Roger and Jo should bring further tongues in that meeting!

17. It is unclear to me whether each individual tongue should be explained, or whether the explanation should wait until further tongues have been brought. Historically, either course of action has been found acceptable. It is not necessary to pause after each tongue for an explanation; there might be one or two more tongues and then one explanation to the set. This demonstrates the great need for the leader to exercise the gift of wisdom before and during every meeting. It does seem, though, that only one person should bring an explanation to each tongue or set of tongues. It is not in order for there to be several attempts at an explanation of the same tongue (verse 27).

18. The gift of tongues must not be suppressed (verse 39).

19. A prayer in tongues should be spoken or sung *euschemonos*. In most versions of the Bible this word is translated as 'decently', but it can be better understood by 'gracefully'. A tongue should not be shouted at great speed, but delivered slowly and beautifully. It is better appreciated if prefixed with a short introduction in English, given either by the leader or the one about to pray (verse 40). For example, the leader could say, 'I think we should now have a few minutes of worship using our spirits instead of our minds. God has given two people a prayer for this service. One will sing his prayer and the other will speak his. They will both use the special language that the Holy Spirit has given to them. When they have finished we will pause for the explanation to their prayers. We have several people

here whom God regularly uses in this way, but if anybody has a vision of prayer or worship, or words of praise or prayer come to them, please speak those out slowly and clearly as that will be the explanation to the tongues.'

20. There should also be a clear *taxis* to the meeting. This is the Greek word which is translated as 'order' or 'arrangement'. Tongues should not be brought haphazardly, but with a deliberate order and arrangement in relation to the other parts of the meeting. The gift of 'wisdom' is crucial. This has prime place in the 1 Corinthians 12 list of spiritual gifts for use in worship. It is this Spirit-given wisdom which determines what should take place next in a particular service. A right understanding and use of 'wisdom' releases the other gifts given for worship and ensures that they are all done gracefully and in order (verse 40).

My personal observation of the current charismatic scene is that spiritual gifts are generally brought in a chaotic free-for-all. Instead of turning to Scripture, leaders appear to model the practice of gifts on their experiences at large 'celebration' meetings. All that I have suggested in this section is being worked out here at Ashburnham amongst ourselves. There has been much embarrassing experimentation in small groups. We continue to correct each other, gently, when we deviate from Scripture. We are beginning to discover the naturalness of gifts and their true beauty as we place them in their rightful home of Christ's body at worship. Please think this section through carefully and then implement your conclusions. Do not allow any disorder to continue—and do not slavishly copy this section! Scripture, not experience or tradition, should mould the pattern of our services.

Tongues in Evangelism

Mark 16:16–17 states, 'And he said to them, "Go out to the whole world; proclaim the Good News to all creation.... These are the signs that will be associated with believers... they will have the gift of tongues."' The purpose of the five signs in this passage is to demonstrate to unbelievers the truth of the proclaimed word and to reveal an insight into the power and glory of the living God. Mark 16:20 adds, 'They, going out, preached everywhere, the Lord working with them and confirming the word by the signs that accompanied it.' These signs, including the gift of tongues, are given for use in serious evangelism.

1 Corinthians 14:22 makes it clear that 'tongues are meant to be a sign not for believers but for unbelievers'. Here Paul reveals that the gift of tongues is that part of Christian worship which will especially challenge unbelievers. These passages suggest a place for tongues in evangelism at two levels: firstly, in the Christian meeting at which unbelievers are present; secondly, in the personal, everyday conversations of Christian believers as they meet, talk and minister to unbelievers. History gives many examples of the latter, but few of the former.

Evangelistic meetings

Harold Horton believed that the gift of tongues should not be used in 'gospel meetings' when it is assumed that unbelievers are present. He reserved the gift for believers' meetings. He argued from 1 Corinthians 14:21 that tongues was a sign to confirm them in their unbelief and is therefore best not used. He testified:

> I recall with pain how I was asked to preach the gospel... before I had a chance to open my lips, the meeting was ruined by eight or ten tongues interpreted as fiery, cutting, judgments of God! What chance has the good tidings in an atmosphere like that?[23]

Whilst this observation was correct, the true solution was not to ban the gift, but to correct its misuse.

The most common objection to using tongues when unbelievers are present is the widespread belief that they will be put off. This is not so. Christians who have been exposed to false teaching about the gift often profess to having been offended by the use of tongues—even quiet, graceful, orderly, worshipful ones! But tongues are not a sign for believers. My experience is that unbelievers are intrigued, tantalized, amazed and curious by the right practice of tongues and explanations. Unbelievers have come to me with more serious questions after these gifts than after a miraculous healing, two or three remarkable prophecies, a spectacular deliverance or 'solid' teaching. Thousands and thousands of unbelievers flocked to the Irvingite meetings in the mid-nineteenth century. Most went to hear the tongues. I do not want to overstate the attractiveness of tongues to unbelievers, but it is a sadly neglected truth. Time and again unbelievers testify that it was the reality of the worship, including tongues, which affected them, more than anything else. It is only when the gift of tongues is abused and misdirected that it is rejected.

An Unusual Tongue

My most unusual experience of tongues and explanations occurred in August 1970. In November 1967 the members of an Ashburnham Bible Research course became convinced that God was promising to revive his people in East Sussex. As a result, from early 1968 the last Monday of each month was set aside to pray for revival in East Sussex.

During the August 1970 meeting, an evangelical Anglican lady received a vision of written words in which was to her an unknown tongue. In her mind she saw a cross with the words *Stat crux dum volvitur orbis* inscribed over the top. She was uncertain what to do as spiritual gifts were then unknown in public meetings at Ashburnham. So she wrote it down and sought out the local vicar in the tea interval.

He instantly recognized the words as excellent Latin, gave the translation, but queried the spelling of *orbis*. He thought it should have been *orbs*. The lady insisted she had seen *orbis* and, overnight, the clergyman realized he had been mistaken about the nominative singular, and that the tongue had been correctly spelt according to classical Latin. The tongue and its translation of 'The cross stands while the world revolves' were read out at the next meeting and attracted considerable interest.

Six weeks later, a local lay reader discovered that this Latin phrase was the centuries old motto of the Carthusian monks, and the Prior of the local order confirmed the incident as a strange evidence of the gift of tongues.

This incident validated tongues to some who had been sceptical. It established the centrality of the cross in renewal as it developed locally, and rebuked the narrowness of the existing vision and prayer. The belief grew that God would bless and renew his whole church, and fellowship replaced suspicion as contact was sought with the Catholic tradition of the church.

Speaking in tongues has been a feature of revival after revival, from monasticism to the present day. Yet, despite this, evangelists often dread somebody praising in tongues at one of 'their' meetings—do they fear they might lose their backers? A major disappointment of the 1984 Mission England series of meetings was the apparent rejection, except for a few new songs, of all that had been learnt in the previous twenty years.

Meanwhile, local churches which do give a right place to spiritual gifts are growing. In those churches where one service is 'charismatic' and one service is 'traditional', it is the former which grows. Serious study shows that in the historic churches this growth is not the result of discontented sheep searching for better pasture, but comes from unbelievers recognizing the reality of the praise.

If the gift of tongues confirms the truth of the proclaimed word and is a sign to unbelievers, it must be nonsense for Christians actively to prevent unbelievers from hearing praise and prayer in tongues. They are the very people who should hear them. The Evil One has successfully hoodwinked a generation of believers into disregarding a potent spiritual weapon. How he must laugh! We would do well to seek and encourage the gift of tongues in more of our meetings—especially when unbelievers are present. It seems absurd to waste so potent a sign. It is my practice to include tongues and explanations in evangelistic meetings and to order them in the way outlined in the previous section for public worship.

Evangelistic conversations

The basic principle for all Christian conversation is that we should be ready to do, or say, exactly what the Spirit prompts. We should initiate nothing. It may be that the Spirit never asks us to use the gift of tongues; or tomorrow he might urge us to offer a demonstration of this supernatural worship and praise. The place of tongues is most usually at the end of a conversation, for the gift is a sign to follow, not precede, the spoken word. It is a common custom to conclude evangelistic conversations with a brief prayer. This is when we can pray in tongues, as well as in English. It is not advisable to burst out in tongues. We should explain what we are about to do, saying for example, 'I think that I should ask the Holy Spirit to help me pray for you. I will not be praying in English but in another special language which God has given to me. Neither you nor I will know what I am praying, but we can be certain that God understands and that the prayer is exactly the right prayer for you.' The gift of explanation does not appear necessary in this setting, as the Bible only stipulates that an explanation is necessary in the public worship and evangelistic services of the church. It is never mentioned in the other New Testament references to the use of the gift of tongues.

The person who has just become a Christian is as vulnerable as a new-born baby. Satan's aim is to extinguish this new life. He has a strategy and ready-made plans for immediate attack. I have found that the use of tongues is most effective in defensive prayer for the new convert. It both thwarts and drives back the Enemy. The best protection is the right use of the name of God; and I often ask a new Christian to read the hymn 'St Patrick's Breastplate', which begins, 'I bind unto myself today the strong Name of the Trinity', making a special prayer of the eighth verse:

> Christ be with me, Christ within me,
> Christ behind me, Christ before me,
> Christ beside me, Christ to win me,
> Christ to comfort and restore me,
> Christ beneath me, Christ above me,
> Christ in quiet, Christ in danger,
> Christ in hearts of all who love me,
> Christ in mouth of friend and stranger.

I then ask the Holy Spirit to inspire my praying and use it to strengthen and protect the new convert. After this brief introduction I often pray in tongues, audibly and confidently, for the new believer. This can be a most moving and meaningful time.

Praying in tongues is frequently used in healing, deliverance and 'inner healing'. These should be part of the evangelistic conversations of the church. In the Gospels, healing and deliverance are inseparable from preaching. The evangelist who preaches the gospel without healing the sick and casting out demons is out of step with Christ and the apostles. It is only the grace of God which brings about the 'success' of such preaching—not its affinity to the biblical practice and pattern. It is a tragedy that most contemporary healings and deliverances are more associated with pastoral care than with evangelistic outreach. Of the forty-four and more people the Scriptures reveal as being healed by prayer, only five at the most can be considered as true believers. The only four recorded probable failures all relate to believers, not unbelievers (Timothy, Paul, Trophimus and Epaphroditus).

It is the same with deliverance and inner healing. The present need for them in the pastoral ministry does not mean that this is their right and natural home. It merely shows that much sub-standard, incomplete evangelism has taken place. It is to be hoped that once all the tidying-up has been done all these aspects of ministry will be restored to evangelism. Prayer in tongues has a particular place in all these 'evangelistic conversations'.

Healing

Prayer is unnecessary if the healing conversation has been initiated directly by God: that is, when an inner prompting of the Spirit has urged us to go to an individual and prophetically announce the arrival of the Lord's healing power. A simple healing command is given: 'Be healed/be open/rise up', etc. I only use prayer in tongues if the healing is slow in coming; or if it appears that God has another work to do which is still unclear; or as praise, after the healing, when English words have been exhausted.

But prayer in tongues is most helpful when the individual has himself requested prayer for healing. In such an instance, it is vital to establish God's will so that vague, aimless prayer is avoided. We need to know whether to announce a healing command, to speak a blessing, to intercede for strength and peace or even to seek a hidden cause for the ailment. The use of tongues is highly recommended whenever God's will is unclear. We can be certain that whenever we use the gift of tongues we are praying according to the mind of God: Romans 8:26–27 make this clear. This should be carefully explained to the individual, for example, we can say, 'I am unsure what it is that God wants to do in your life, so I am going to ask the Holy Spirit to pray for you, through me. He will use another language and, though we will not understand what I pray, it will be exactly right for you.' It is my experience that the Lord's will becomes much clearer after a time of prayer in tongues. As already mentioned, the gift of explanation is not necessary in this setting. Some people consider the guidance that often follows such prayer in tongues to be the explanation, but I think the guidance is the answer to the prayer, not its explanation.

Deliverance

Many do not recommend the use of tongues in this context because the demonic reaction can at times be quite violent. The sound of heavenly praise is abhorrent to the foul forces of the Evil One. But I have found exorcistic focused prayer in tongues to be most helpful in dislodging difficult demons. Praise in tongues appears to help speed the process along as it frequently forces a demon to reveal itself. Once the demonized person has been set free by Jesus and brought to faith, I suggest that tongues be part of the 'St Patrick's

Breastplate' type prayers for them (see page 46).

Inner healing

This American phrase is a misnomer. I prefer 'binding up the broken-hearted' as it is more biblical. It describes guiding an individual into the reality of the Father God's forgiveness and love. This is a sensitive, discreet and gentle ministry. Prayer in tongues is, at times, like the cooing of the divine dove and is much gentler and more discreet than English. It should be used in a similar way as for healing and deliverance. If the person is a believer and already has received this gift they should be encouraged to use it. In praise they naturally draw near to God and are embraced by his love.

Conclusion

The use of tongues in evangelism is essentially that of a sign. It demonstrates that a supernatural God has broken through; it drives back the Evil One; it enables vital guidance to be received. This use of tongues must be rediscovered, for God's sake and for the world's sake. There are a considerable number of well-attested incidents when an unbeliever has known the language of the tongue and has been converted as a result. We need to take courage and be ready to use tongues as part of our evangelism. Who knows what God will do through this precious prayer and praise? We must never forget again that the gift of tongues is for unbelievers.

An Evidence of Spirit-Baptism

The gift of tongues is but one of several evidences which demonstrate that an individual has been filled with Holy Spirit. Others, all more important, are a change in appearance: Acts 2:33, Acts 6:15, 2 Corinthians 3:7–18; an increase in appetite for spiritual matters: Acts 2:42–46, Acts 4:32–35; experiencing a time of extreme attack, be it temptation, suffering or persecution: Mark 1:12–13, Romans 8:17–23; an overwhelming assurance of salvation: Romans 8:15–17, Hebrews 10:15; and, most important of all, a dramatic increase in power for witness: Luke 24:48–49, Acts 1:4–8, 4:31, 6:10, 9:20–22, 10:46, 19:6–10, 1 Thessalonians 1:5, Hebrews 2:4. All of these evidences should be continuous. They begin at the moment when the person is sealed/anointed/filled with Holy Spirit, but they ought not to cease. In water baptism the candidate descends into the baptistry, is immersed, then comes up and out and is towelled dry. But the candidate in Spirit baptism goes down into the baptistry of the Holy Spirit, is immersed by Jesus in the river of living water, and is meant to stay there. We should remain by obedience in that baptistry, evermore being filled, like a sponge soaking up the water in a bath. (See the Ashburnham Insight book *Baptized in Holy Spirit*.)

It can be no evidence of our present state of Spirit fullness to say, 'I used to pray in tongues'; or 'Six months ago I did some witnessing'; or, 'I used to read the Scriptures avidly'; or, 'I am not really sure whether God loves me'. The gift of tongues is meant to be a continuous evidence of a permanent state. That is not to pretend that we never, because of disobedience and weakness, leave the baptistry. I do frequently. But the grace of God is such that we can always return. Many times in the past I have neglected to pray in tongues for months on end. However, I know of nobody from whom the gift has been withdrawn. Once saved, always saved. Once a tongue speaker, always a tongue speaker. We might not be living in the present benefit of our salvation, and might not be actually praying in tongues, but the permanent potential exists from the moment the gift is first received. It can be inferred from 1 Corinthians 14:15 that the percentage of our prayers in tongues should be near the percentage of our prayers in English. Many find it essential to pray in tongues every day. Some sing in tongues whilst driving, others whilst doing the housework, or menial tasks. We will one day be called to account for our stewardship of this precious gift. Paul mentioned his huge quantity of tongues—more than all the Corinthians! The gift of tongues can be used in every area of prayer—in thanksgiving, confession, petition, adoration, supplication, intercession, praise, etc. However, there appear to me to be six areas where, if we are living in the Spirit, tongues will naturally overflow and be seen as an evidence of our dwelling place.

Worship

When we are at worship the gift of tongues helps us to express our love for Jesus in a much better way than mere human language. We struggle in human relationships to find a more creative and meaningful way of saying 'I love you' for the ninety-ninth time. In our divine relationship the gift of tongues does this more beautifully, more aptly, than mere human artistry could ever attain.

Intercession

The gift of tongues is especially valuable in intercession when we do not know what to pray. 'The Spirit comes to help us in our weakness,' said Paul in Romans 8:26, and we might well add 'and in our ignorance'. We are often asked, or prompted, to pray for Mr Smith and have no conception of his needs. Then it is time for tongues. The Spirit will intercede through us, according to the mind of God.

Breakthrough

The gift of tongues helps in the achievement of spiritual breakthroughs. Replies to prayer are often slow in coming, either due to demonic opposition, or because God is pressing patience and perseverance into our lives. When our faith is low because of the delay, we should pray with the spirit. God's faith is never low, and it is our spirits that are in tune with this sort of faith. In impossible situations, when opposition is great or circumstances are grim, our prayers can easily become statements of doubt. These are the moments when the gift of tongues is so helpful. Prayer in tongues is full of God's faith. It is full of his self-confidence.

Lamentation

This gift can be used to articulate sadness. My generation does not find prayer lamentation easy. For some reason we have a problem lamenting to God. How can we pour out our anguish over events like Aberfan, an earthquake, a plane crash, a terrorist bomb, mass starvation? How do we share in God's agony? We have not been taught to lament. Prayer in tongues can be a very meaningful lamentation about the unspeakable horrors of a world reaping the ghastly results of sin and God's judgement.

Thanksgiving

How can English express adequate gratitude at the conversion of a wayward son, or the healing of a close friend?

'Thank you' appears beggarly. I find a loud burst in tongues is much better. I know then that I have said 'thank you' properly. The gift of tongues has a special place in thanksgiving.

Preparation

The gift of tongues builds us up. It is the experience of many that regular, frequent, consistent praying in tongues has played a significant part in transforming them from people with an ineffective witness into people whose witness brings lasting results. I sang in tongues for at least three-quarters of an hour a day for four months to lull our twins to sleep. There was no noticeable improvement in their sleep pattern, but lots of people commented on a marked change in me! Perhaps prayer in tongues, like fasting, is the spiritual equivalent to press-ups.

The gift of tongues is recommended when we know a specific conversation or meeting will take place and are unsure how to proceed. Uncertain intercession is next to useless. This gift is for those times when we are unclear as to God's will. We should pray in tongues, at length, focused on the person with whom we will be speaking. It does appear we can focus, or direct, our praying in tongues. The praying is with our spirit, and the directing is with our mind. We visualize the individual in our 'mind's eye', then begin to pray in tongues for him. Some people find it helpful to preface their tongue with a short prayer in English which explains the intended direction of the tongue. This is neither magic, nor manipulation, but rather accurate, effective intercession. It is the experience of many that this discipline, in conjunction with prayer in their own language and fasting, brings results that are not otherwise seen.

Gillian Warren—a member of St Mary's, Barcombe, E. Sussex

Gillian, the wife of a Sussex landowner, received the gift of tongues in 1969 and has regularly employed it for the last sixteen years. She uses the gift many times a day, for praise, loving, warfare and intercession, and appears to have been given three quite different languages to meet these varied needs.

She says, 'From time to time, when Jesus seems very close, I yearn to hug him to express love for him in a human way. Clearly this is not possible. So I ask him for a special love-language which will really delight his heart and tell him truly how much I love him. This he always gives.

'Sometimes, when I am praying for a particular situation where evil abounds and demonic beings need rebuking, a much rougher, more guttural, language comes, which is only present at times of spiritual warfare.

'The "normal" tongue, which I use on and off during the day, serves for intercession as well as for praise. I use it when driving, praying privately, listening on the telephone, when others are praying or I am beginning to minister to anyone. Whenever I do not know how or what to pray, I pray with my spirit. Often, a picture or other clue will emerge in my mind which enables me to pray in English very specifically.

'This language also comes in emergencies. When our daughter rang to say that her baby son had died, I immediately prayed in this particular tongue. My instinctive reaction when a difficult moment arises, during a service or business meeting, is to pray with my spirit. The same thing happens whenever my children are ill, have pains or nightmares, or when I get frightened.

'I am so thankful to have been given these languages. They are a constant source of encouragement, strength and blessing.'

Singing with the spirit

The present charismatic movement, both within and without the historic churches, misunderstands many things about congregational singing with the spirit. This is exemplified by the use of the term 'singing in the Spirit'—meaning in the Holy Spirit. As already mentioned, all singing, like all praying, should be 'in the Spirit' whether it be in tongues or in English. But only singing and praying in tongues can be described as 'with the spirit'—meaning with the human spirit.

It must be realized that most contemporary singing with the spirit is embryonic. We have not yet got it right. Though at times it may be heavenly and at others deeply moving, this should not stop us from re-evaluating this phenomenon and attempting to root its practice more securely in Scripture and history. No man can speak with authority on this matter. My thoughts are only given as tentative suggestions. But it seems to me that there are three areas which require more study, prayer and experimentation.

Spontaneity

There seems to be an unspoken understanding that singing with the spirit should be spontaneous. One moment we are singing in English and then we mysteriously find ourselves singing in tongues. It just happens! This is a false supra-supernatural understanding of the charismata. 1 Corinthians 14:26 indicates that guidance about gifts ought to be sought before a meeting. When singing in tongues is on God's menu for the meeting, he is surely keen to inform us more than two seconds before it is due.

Earlier this morning (I don't normally believe these sentences in other books, but this is quite true) the wife of the chaplain at a local Methodist girls' private school telephoned me. She said she believed God had given her the task of introducing and leading a time of singing with the spirit at our next public meeting. I, or another, will say, 'And now, Christine will lead us into singing with the spirit.' What is 'unspiritual' about this?

On another occasion we might say, 'At the end of this next song we will sing the tune again, but this time in tongues.' It is not deemed spiritually subnormal for one to lead into a chorus and the rest to follow, or for another to announce a hymn and there is no biblical passage which supports the idea that singing with the spirit must be spontaneous.

Harmonies

In the 1960s most corporate singing in tongues was 'melodic'. By this I mean it had a structure and rhythm, even a tune with different parts. This was especially so in those groups affiliated to Pastor North—one of the earliest of groupings of house churches. It was also a particular feature of renewal in Sweden.

During the 1970s singing in tongues became more harmonic without, except on rare occasions, an obvious tune. Some suggest this 'harmonic' singing is based on the structure of five notes, called the pentatonic mode (which was widely used in times past and dates back to at least 2000 B.C.), and is a primitive form of singing arising from a deep subconscious musicality in all people. This, perhaps, is why singing with the spirit is so liberating for non-musical people. Others hear an echo of plainsong in congregational singing in tongues and enter into a new appreciation of different traditions in worship. Many have only had experience of 'harmonic' singing and falsely assume this is how it is always meant to be. There is tremendous scope for development.

We began, recently, to ask the Lord not just to give us words, but also a tune; to move us from personal praise en masse, to the body of Christ corporately worshipping with our spirits and presenting a united song to God. We began by singing a known English melody and practised holding that melody whilst singing in tongues. Then, with much embarrassment, we commenced singing corporate melodic tongues. These are stronger and more structured. There is more bass and less soprano. After a few months of experimentation we found non-musical people developing the confidence truly to 'sing' with the spirit, instead of 'chanting' with the spirit. I would suggest that small groups take time prayerfully to experiment and develop this lovely gift within their local church.

Explanations

It is normal today to consider 'singing with the spirit' to be personal praise en masse and therefore not in need of any explanation. Bishop David Pytches defended this in *Renewal* magazine, by asserting that, 'An interpretation is not necessary because all are addressing God. No one interpretation would be adequate in such a case.'[24] However, 1 Corinthians 14 seems to indicate that all public tongues should be explained. Many ask, 'Whose tongue is explained?' The answer is that there is unity in singing with the spirit, whether melodic or harmonic, and it is this 'overall' song, or common theme, which is explained. When a congregation of two hundred is singing with the spirit there are not two hundred different songs, all needing a separate explanation—that would be chaos. Instead, there is one song being sung in two hundred different languages, or, rather, one theme being put in two hundred different ways. This is why only one explanation is needed.

We have already noted that an interpretation is not a translation. It is the explanation of the gist or theme. It is my experience that God does give an explanation—and frequently this is in the form of a vision of creation. The explanation may be a psalm, an already known song, a Spirit-directed new solo in English, a preceding hymn, a spoken prayer or praise, a dance or a vision.

Some suggest that the Hebrew word *selah* which appears frequently in the psalms represented a congregational pause to allow the musicians to play 'theme music' relevant to the psalm. Perhaps singing with the spirit is the *selah* in a meeting. It often sounds more like an orchestra playing than a choir singing. *Finlandia,* the *Pastoral* symphony, the *Planets* suite all call to mind a picture of creation. During—or before—a time of singing with the spirit, one individual may receive from God a glorious vision of his creation being set free from its slavery to decadence. This vision should be described in detail and recognized as the explanation. Leaders need the courage and freedom to experiment in this area and to allow this precious gift to mature among their people. Experimentation in small groups is desirable before launching out with a congregation of several hundred.

The gift of tongues develops from sounds to language; the gift of healing from coughs to cancer; so too the gift of explanations develops in individuals as they gain confidence, learn to listen more attentively to the Spirit, and are given the freedom in which to make mistakes. Eventually you will discover that the corporate sung tongue and explanation will often be the climax of a church service.

Starting to Pray in Tongues

The following guidance is for those who have never prayed in tongues and now wish to receive this gift. Prayer in tongues is only for those regenerated believers in Christ who have been filled with Holy Spirit. The Spirit is received in one of two ways. Either Jesus pours out the Spirit upon an individual without a human intermediary, or the Spirit is received through the laying on of hands. The latter rite is for those believers who have either been baptized in water, or are about to be baptized in water. (For a fuller discussion see the Ashburnham Insight book *Baptized in Holy Spirit*.) Those in doubt should follow Luke 11:1–13 and keep on asking, seeking and knocking for the Holy Spirit. If you are unsure about this, please ask the leaders of your church to talk with you, lay hands on you and pray with you for the anointing with Holy Spirit.

If you are to receive this gift, you must surely believe there is such a thing as speaking in tongues. It might be helpful to ask a friend to give a demonstration of spoken and sung tongues—especially if you are worried about losing control. You also need to believe that tongues is for you. Some people have the fatalistic notion that, 'If God wants me to speak in tongues, he'll make sure I do.' God does unexpectedly give this gift to a few who do not ask, but

My Own Story

I first met people who claimed to pray in tongues in 1972, but as I only ever heard secretive muttering or shrill screaming, I assumed it was ecstatic and valueless. However, as those I knew placed great value on tongues, I surreptitiously purchased under-the-counter copies of *Nine O'clock in the Morning*[25] and *The Holy Spirit and You.*[26]

In 1973 a desire grew in me for Spirit baptism. I understood tongues as something distasteful, but necessary for this experience—like eating my sprouts up before I could have pudding. I was apprehensive, but curious. For several consecutive nights in December 1973 I informed God that I would not go to sleep until he filled me with his Spirit. Morning after morning I woke disappointed. But in the early morning of December 31st I was gloriously filled whilst under the bed covers.

I found myself tentatively whispering in tongues (I dreaded lest my parents hear!) and was amazed to discover I could stop, start and even vary the speed at will. I tiptoed downstairs to the toilet, pulled the chain and established volume control whilst the cistern emptied. Was I the only person alive with such tongue control? It was several years before I found my tongue was normal.

I used tongues occasionally for five years, assuming it had some point, but with no idea what that was. I travelled extensively in 1978 and heard someone recommend singing in tongues for use while driving. This was an instant success. I cannot remember songs, and tongues was better than 'la la'. Light dawned. Tongues had meaning. It was worship. I began to study and soon realized, experimented with and appreciated other uses. Since then I have prized this precious gift more and more highly. Friends sometimes say that I am good with words, but I would not be without my unlearnt, unknown language.

normally those who receive are those who have kept on asking.

You should ask the Holy Spirit to give you this gift and then you should receive it by faith. Faith is not persuading yourself about the truth of tongues. Faith is letting the truth about tongues persuade you. Normally when we exercise faith about something it means we have no experience as immediate evidence. If we did, it would be sight and not faith. Both you and the Holy Spirit have a part in praying with tongues. Acts 2:4 states, 'They...began to speak in foreign languages as the Spirit gave them the gift of speech.' The Holy Spirit does not provide lips or breath as his part of the package. Your function is to disentangle your mind from your vocal chords, to take a breath and trust the Lord, and to form your lips into a word. Then begin to speak that word, trusting the Spirit to give the following words. Some people start immediately with a complete language. Others stay at an elemental stage for several weeks. Many agonize for months, persistently asking, seeking and knocking, before they pray in tongues. There is, as with all aspects of the Christian life, much sweat and little glory. Patience, perseverance and obedience are the keys to faith and maturity.

As soon as you receive this gift doubts will start to come your way. The Evil One will sow immediate disbelief in a frantic attempt to silence the adoration of God flowing from your lips. He has great success with two lies. Firstly, 'You are making it up.' Take comfort. Everybody who has ever spoken in tongues has heard this lie, yet few people possess the ability to create a new foreign language. The gift of tongues is for most their first experience of hearing God speak directly through them. It is always much more natural and 'everyday' than they expected. If you remain unpersuaded, ask a tongue speaking leader to listen and advise.

The second doubt will be, 'It is not a language, it is gibbering rubbish.' All have suffered the agony of this demonic doubt. The truth is that all foreign languages sound gibberish. I live in a multi-national community where French, German, Italian, Spanish, Finnish, and other exotic languages can all be heard on any day of the week. Believe me, all foreigners sound like raving idiots, especially when excited. All my scepticism about tongues vanished after a few weeks here!

The best advice is to seek reassurance from a tongue-speaking leader. He should guide you along the glorious road of praise from the first faltering sounds to complete maturity in your God-given language of prayer.

Once you have begun to speak in tongues, it is good to spend time, privately, singing in tongues as well. This can be most liberating. Many people find it far easier to start and develop their language by singing, rather than speaking. Experiment with both and see which is most helpful. As far as possible, continue to pray and praise in tongues every day. Seek God for the gift of explanation. Ask God whether you should use either of these gifts in public worship. Your gift of tongues is to help you praise the holy name of God more fully. Make good use of it.

The fastest growing church the world has ever seen is the Full Gospel Church in Seoul, Korea. This church has grown from nobody to half a million members in twenty-six years. Pastor Paul Yonggi Cho, its leader, says this about tongues: 'I am convinced every Christian who desires it, can ask for it, and receive it.'

Hooray and hallelujah for the glorious gift of tongues!

Notes

1. Morton T. Kelsey, *Tongue Speaking* (Hodder & Stoughton 1968).
2. Harold Horton, *The Gifts of the Spirit* (Assemblies of God Publishing House 1934).
3. Edward D. O'Connor, *A Catholic Pentecostal Movement* (in *Ave Maria* 105, No. 22 June 3, 1967), p.8.
4. David du Plessis, *Glossolalia* (A privately printed tract. No. 3 in a series of 6, 1971), p.4.
5. Tertullian, *The Ante-Nicene Fathers*, Vol. 3, by Cleveland Coxe (Eerdmans 1951), p.446.
6. Harold Horton, *The Gifts of the Spirit* (Assemblies of God Publishing House 1934), p.166ff.
7. David Pytches, *Answers to Almost Every Question about the Gift of Tongues* (in *Renewal* magazine, No. 113, October 1984).
8. Michael Green, *I Believe in Satan's Downfall* (Hodder & Stoughton 1981), p.231.
9. Rene Laurentin, *Catholic Pentecostalism* (Darton, Longman & Todd 1977), p.69.
10. Rene Laurentin *op. cit.* p.70.
11. Morton Kelsey, *Tongue Speaking* (Hodder & Stoughton 1968), p.50.
12. James Packer, *Keep in Step with the Spirit* (Inter-Varsity Press 1984), p.209.

13. Irenaeus, *The Ante-Nicene Fathers,* Vol. 1, by Cleveland Coxe (Eerdmans 1951), p.531.
14. Novatian, *The Ante-Nicene Fathers,* Vol. 5, by Cleveland Coxe (Eerdmans 1951), p.641.
15. Chrysostom, quoted in Morton Kelsey *Tongue Speaking* (Hodder & Stoughton 1968), p.40.
16. Augustine, *The Fathers of the Church,* Vol. 24 by Joseph Defferari (The Catholic University of America Press n.d.), p.445.
17. Frederick Conybeare, *Encyclopedia Britannica* 11th edition, Vol. 27 (Cambridge University Press 1910), p.10.
18. Teresa of Avila, *The Collected Works of St Teresa of Avila* by Kienan Kavanaugh (ICS Publications 1976), p.109.
19. William Burrough, quoted in Morton Kelsey *Tongue Speaking* (Hodder & Stoughton 1968), p.55.
20. Thomas Walsh, quoted in Michael Harper *As at the Beginning* (Hodder & Stoughton 1965), p.21.
21. Quoted in Bernard Bresson *Studies in Ecstasy* (Vantage Press 1966), p.86.
22. Harold Horton, *The Gifts of the Spirit* (Assemblies of God Publishing House 1934), p.168.
23. *Ibid.*
24. David Pytches, *Answers to Almost Every Question about the Gift of Tongues* (in *Renewal* magazine, No. 113, October 1984), p.8.
25. Dennis J. Bennett, *Nine O'Clock in the Morning* (Kingsway Publications 1970).
26. Dennis & Rita Bennett, *The Holy Spirit and You* (Kingsway Publications 1971).